Romanian Gypsies

9 True Stories about What it's Like To Be a Gypsy in Romania

by Catalin Gruia

37-Minutes Publishing

First Printing, July 2013

Translated by Andreea Geambasu

Cover design by Tudor Smalenic

Cover photo by Bogdan Croitoru

Proof reading by Alexandra Popescu

ISBN-13: 978-1492994671

ISBN-10: 1492994677

ALSO BY CATALIN GRUIA

The Man They Killed on Christmas Day

The Rise and Fall of Saxon Transylvania

What About Dracula? Romania's
Schizophrenic Dilemma

Who Were The Dacians?

Contents

Foreword

*W*herever you are in Romania, – in any city or village –, if you take a 30-minute walk in any direction, you'll find a community of poor Gypsies.

Apart from a minority that got rich exploiting barely-legal economic opportunities, for more than two thirds of some one million Romanian Gypsies, the tumultuous years following the fall of communism meant a transition towards hopeless poverty, delinquency, and violence.

They were among the first laid off during the 1990s restructuring process and many did not manage to get rehired. About 70% of the Gypsies live on a Minimum Income Guarantee (financial aid from the State) and occasional activities. 80% of them have no profession.

Like Mocirla ("The Swamp"), almost every poor Gypsy community is affected by the same "shortages" when it comes to jobs, income, education, access to medical services, identity cards, property titles, and miserable, dirty, overcrowded houses.

This is a story about what it's like to be a Gypsy (Roma) in Romania. A story told by the Gypsies themselves.

Over 16 hours of interviews were edited for concision and clarity. Certain regionalisms, flagrant language and grammar mistakes were straightened out, here and there.

About This Book

*H*ere we are: two city boys from the Capital lost in Bacau's countryside train station in a downpour, waiting and waiting and waiting. "Call her", photographer Bogdan Croitoru finally tells me. The phone rings again and again and again...

Not a chance. Not only did the lady with whom we've been in contact – and who was supposed to introduce us to the Gypsy community in Mocirla, Buhusi – wasn't waiting for us at the station as agreed, but she also had her phone turned off.

Eventually, we bought some rubber boots and raincoats (it was raining so heavily that the water had risen in the streets), and began wandering around the city. I don't remember how we got to a school where there was some sort of a craft exhibition by Roma children from various schools in the area.

There we met Gabi, the Roma language teacher at the school in Mocirla. We told her who we were and what we wanted to do and, unbelievably – the previous series of misfortunes proved to be a wonderful opportunity – Gabi took us to her house and so we were able (when we had no hope left) to enter and be accepted by the community we wanted to study. The great opportunity of this story was that things didn't work out as planned.

I wanted to tell the story of what is it like to be a Roma (Gypsy) in Romania. But to tell the Gypsies' story you have to become one. And in Romania this is easier said than done.

When a Romanian calls you "Gypsy", his lips distort in a contemptuous grimace: he wants to say you're a thief, you're lazy and dirty… Most Romanians are tolerant of foreigners, but the Gypsies are considered inferior, someone you don't want to be around. A recent study shows that 75% of Romanians don't want to live near a Gypsy community.

Here are five important trends that emerged after Ceausescu's fall in 1989, when the Gypsy issue emerged in a whole new perspective in the Romanian society:

• Rise of an active ethnic and political movement among the Roma,

• Enrichment of a small segment of the Roma population through the use of "almost" legal economic opportunities,

• The growing impoverishment of the majority of Gypsies without any hope of correction,

• Growing delinquency and violence,

• Outburst of conflict between groups of Romanians and Roma people.

Gypsies were often the first to be laid-off from jobs in the early 1990s, and have been among those most persistently blocked from re-entering the labour force. Labour market exclusion perpetuates the poverty cycle and lowers living standards.

Many Roma have limited future opportunities to climb out of poverty due to low development conditions and long-standing discrimination - including lack of education, poor health and limited opportunities for participating in social and political life.

The Gypsies are a very heterogeneous population. There are Roma people in 262 towns and 2.686 townships, in 40 Romanian counties. How can you choose a representative Gypsy community as a model? Yet all the Gypsy communities are affected by the same problems - lack of jobs, income, education, access to medical services, IDs, property rights, overcrowded residential areas, etc.

I was convinced that, in a small Gypsy community chosen on scientific sociological criteria, all the issues affecting the larger Gypsy community could be found. For example, from the small village school one can infer the story of the Gypsy education. The rich of the village can stand for that minority of Gypsies who gathered incredible wealth in the troubled years after Ceausescu's fall. The one arrested by the village Police can speak about Gypsy delinquency. And so on.

I ended up choosing Mocirla (the Swamp), on the outskirts of Romanian town Buhusi, on completely subjective grounds. There are hundreds of cases in Romania in which Gypsies are isolated and isolate themselves. What drew me here was a name that stroked me in a sociological report: one of Mocirla's unofficial leaders was named Catalin Gruia. My name! I took it as a sign that I had to go there. I had to meet „Bursucu" ("The Badger") – the Gypsy Catalin Gruia – and we did not like each other at all. He was on the side of those Mocirlans who were wary of the fact that my name was also Gruia…

13

I forgot to tell you that I was shocked to discover that half of Mocirla is named Gruia. And if at first I thought this matching of names would be an advantage – I quickly became everyone's "cousin" – during the last few days, it backfired. People at the bar were starting to say that we weren't really journalists – photographer Bogdan Croitoru and me – but "spies" from Bucharest and that we want to overthrow Nae Butuc, the community's unofficial leader. (Gabi had a smoldering conflict with the informal leaders of the community, who called us to the tavern to find out what was up with us...)

All this happened as some Mocirlans would have liked to find a young Gypsy king with connections in Bucharest to solve their problems. All the prerequisites are in place for such a man to come along, raised in the community or returning from Italy, able to unite them all and transform a bunch of firewood thieves into a real organized mafia.

Fast forward. Almost 6 years have passed...

Stressed out and whiny as I am, I couldn't fully appreciate the time spent in Mocirla. But today, I often remember the beautiful moments spent there: the days I would wake up at 5 a.m. to wash up using dew from the black locust flowers on the street (after several days of not having any means to wash, you take desperate measures), or being shown around the community by Tatiana, the about 12 years old blonde Gypsy girl, whose songs and zest for life were utterly contagious; Bogdan's generosity, who was bitten raw and was allergic to the fleas on the mats, had sacrificed himself by sleeping on the floor, leaving me, the delicate one, the bed; Steaua's last game of the season, discussed with our host's little sister - beautiful, well-behaved and obliging like a Japanese girl from the Samurai era.

Nine True Stories

*H*ow was Limbos ("Tongue-y") to know that that night would be different? He came down from the hill, talked a bit with some friends by the road, walked into a Cristi Teslaru boutique, the only one in the neighborhood, and stole a pack of underwear. He gave away eight of the pairs to people on the street, like a modern-day Robin Hood, and brought two pairs home to his wife. All this fun cost him two years in prison. Upon his return to Mocirla, he stole a chicken (snapping the neck of another irritating bird and leaving it in the coop) and went back to jail for another year.

At 24, Limbos, whose real name is Ciprian Gruia, spent four years in prison and three years in school, two of which he completed in prison. He's a strange young man with quiet, slick, black eyes, a gentle voice that gets caught in his thin mustache, a sandy-blonde curl hanging in the middle of his forehead, a lot of enemies, and restless hands and feet. He had three little children. Now he has one. He found the last one lying dead in bed next to him and buried him.

To the rest of the world, Mocirla is infamous as a thieve nest. To Limbos, it's home. Outsiders who see Mocirla's nearly 200 run-down houses, spread out randomly like a sick swarm of bees on a hill on the outskirts of Buhusi, watching them from their cars while driving to Roman, raise their eyebrows and speed up. Townspeople are afraid to climb up here: most Gypsies have empty bellies, sly gazes, sharp tongues, and quick hands. Every time it rains – and it often does – the mud reaches the knees, and the three roads that climb up from Orbic Street towards the Gypsies, with a 55-degree slope inaccessible to cars, literally turn into mud slides.

None of the nearly 1,000 Roma living on the hill has a job. A few hundred left for Italy and are sending money back home. Those left behind live off stealing, welfare, state child support, and occasional suspicious jobs. Most of the men have been to jail.

This school year, 220 of the 260 children enrolled in the Buhusi Arts and Crafts school in the Orbic neighborhood are from the Roma community. During the farming season, the majority leave school to work in the fields with their parents. When they come to school, they get bored quickly and leave, unable to be kept in class by any means. Once they reach 16, many abandon school as they're getting married or starting to work.

Until a few years ago, Mocirlans worked in the felt factory in Buhusi. After the factory's restructuring, they were left to get by however they could. They are all waiting for a Messiah with a different face (a second Ceausescu to resuscitate the country, or at least a patron with a lot of money to revive the factory, or an Andreea Marin to bring them on her philanthropic talk show "Surprises, Surprises" and give them what they need). Mocirla cannot be understood from the outside. You have to go inside. You have to meet the people who live here.

1

The Unemployed Man

*V*asile Gruia, 56 years old, with 9 kids, a
wise man among the Gypsies, talkative,
charming, a 10th grade graduate, a former
painter in a factory for 31 years. He didn't teach his
children Romani because he's convinced it won't
help them with anything. He lives on welfare and
odd day jobs.

Man, before, in the communist days, if they
found out you didn't have a job, they'd force one on
you! They'd give you a job. You'd have something
to live on. But now, nobody asks you, "Man, where
do you get your money from? How do you live?
What do you do?"

Now people just begin stealing, or do whatever they can. I wouldn't steal, even though I'm tempted by need. Not me, 'cause I don't do that, 'cause I make it on the little I have, but there are families with seven, eight little kids, and when they start crying from hunger, their parent or grandparent or brother will say, "Come on, man, let's do something, anything, but let's cash in!" And they'll steal something and get seven, eight, ten years in prison.

Here...start at this end of Mocirla and go all the way to the other side, and stop at every house and ask if anyone has a job. No one. What are they supposed to live on? They start stealing 'cause they don't have anything else to do.

There's some forest nearby. There are some who have horses. They'll go to the forest and steal a cartful of wood. If it wasn't for them, this whole area you see, and there are another two or three villages – Silistea, Romani, Lipoveni – if it wasn't for them, bringing carts of wood to sell here and there, 'cause they sell it cheaper, I don't even know how these people would heat their houses.

Even here, we whine and complain, but there are villages, even farther away from the cities...you should see them. They shake at the sight of a coin. It's hard in this country, really hard!

Don't you see how people with an education, the brighter ones, all leave Romania? To America, to Italy, to Australia. Everywhere. They leave and that's where they end up. 'Cause they didn't know how to value them over here. A doctor here gets five million lei (150$). And shouldn't he ask you for money when you go to him? Of course he should, 'cause a doctor can't get by on five million (150$) a month. A policeman gets seven, eight million (240$) and he has to deal with all those crazies. He can get killed at any time, 'cause there are dangerous people.

They'll come out in front of you, and you, as a criminal, say to yourself, "well, better his mom be the one crying, and not mine," and you kill him. Or he kills you. Here in Mocirla policemen shot people. And what happened to them? Who knows? Three people were shot. It was fatal, not "oh, I was defending myself." He shot straight at them. What happened, man? If it's a law for me that means it's a law for everyone. 'Cause like they say, the law is everyone's mother...

I was a painter in a factory. And I worked in the factory for 31 years. Can you imagine? Thirty-one years in the same job. Since the day I started until unemployment. They gave us those compensation salaries: they didn't take into account your ability to work, they didn't take into account your qualifications. It only mattered if you were one of the boss' guys. Now I don't even have a pension 'cause I'm not old enough. I have to wait to turn 62. I have that tiny welfare, and, to be honest, without any shame, I'll go here and there and work by the day. There are lots of people that no one will hire. Out of fear. They'll say, "This guy will see what I have in my yard and come and steal it." So they'll only take people they know have never had any problems with the police.

So, you get it. Nothing can get done here. If only there was some company to give them work. If not, it's going to go on like this until the shit hits the fan. The police can't do anything to them, the government can't do anything to them, no one. They'd rather go to jail than hear their hungry kids crying at home.

Look at me: at my age, I tried to work on construction sites. In Bacau and Buhusi, I went to all the construction sites possible. I've been out of a job for two years. No one will take me. I'm over 50. I can't even find any work „under the counter". And with the minimum state welfare...why do they even give me those two million? They make me sit around for almost twenty days, and don't give me anything to produce, something that I can benefit from producing, so I can get my minimum wage?

There's a guy on the field who clocks you in. But if you go and see the job these boys do there, you'll die laughing. They take a paper from over here, put it over there, hang out over there, and then they send them home and write down four hours.

Give me something to do, man!

2

The Schoolgirl

*L*et's say her name is Geanina. She climbs a
hill, through the mud, and sings soulfully:
"Man, life slips away and all that's waiting
for us is a cold grave/Once you're gone, you're
forgotten by everyooooooooone!" This girl is the devil
herself. "She has green eyes, she's blonde, she loves
life, she goes around with boys 10, 15 years older
than her," says one of her classmates, Cora, who got
married when she was 13.

Geanina, an only child, is 14, she's in the
sixth grade, and this was probably her last year of
school. She's going to get married soon, but only
"with a Gypsy like me, so I have something to talk to
him about." Here, if a girl reaches ninth grade and
isn't married, people yell "old maid!" at her. She has

had 10 boyfriends. She dumped the last one because she saw him with another girl.

„I didn't leave him because he's poor. I left him because he doesn't know how to respect me. If he respects me, I'll respect him too. When I got to school, I saw him with another girl. You choose: me or her. And he chose her. But I'm not mad. I'm not his boss. The kid does what he wants. These days I don't go to school much because dad and mom go off and work by the day, and I stay home so no one steals our stuff. Actually, you know, I don't go to school anymore because the boys kidnap you. They kidnap girls around here. If a boy sees a girl he likes, him and his friends kidnap her, they take her somewhere, he sleeps with her, and it's done, the girl is married.

They tried to take me once. The boys came to school on horseback, they run us down... He rode in with his friends and took me. I barely got away. I begged him! They dragged me like this. They took me to his house. I was lucky he let me go when my friends Monica and Lacramioara came.

3

The Sick Lady

Margareta Avadanei, 49 years old, has a huge tumor on her left leg. She sits in her house like a monstrous doll that her scrawny husband moves from the window to the bed and back. He washes her and takes care of her. She had 400,000 lei (12$) help from the state that the mayor withdrew when records proved that her husband, Vasile, had received a 200,000 lei (6$) raise on his pension. She takes a fistful of painkillers, but they don't have any effect anymore. She cries and her voice shakes when she tells her story.

What if I could at least go to the outhouse? What would that be like?! I lie on the bed and I can't do anything. If this good husband of mine turns me over, I turn. If not, I don't. It's hard. I can't go outside. Who will take me out? I stay in the house…my elbows are black from the windowsill. In the morning, he puts me by the window, just like this, all day. I can't take the pain anymore.

I've been like this for 20 years. It started out like a rash. Then it started to grow. And it kept swelling up. Like blisters after you burn your skin. When I'd go to the hospital, they'd treat me, they'd give me some of that spray that heals. But now it doesn't heal anymore. No hospital will even take me anymore. I keep going, but none will take me. They can't do anything for me. And treatments are expensive.

I don't have anything, no pension, no state help. Vasile has a medical pension. Money? From where? I borrowed money from a loan shark, and I'm in debt eight million lei (240$). I get four, I give back eight. Where am I supposed to get eight million from to pay them back? It's a hard life for me, very hard.

Where else can I go? They come and ask me, "Are you going to give us the money or not?" Where am I supposed to get it from? Vasile has a hole the size of a coin in his head. And with his stomach, and his bile, the poor guy. For a man to live with this kind of torture every day – it's hard. Another man wouldn't put up with everything I've been through. It'd be hard for him...

Where else can I go? Who can else can I talk to? When my parents were alive, I had some support, but now... my parents are dead. Where else can I go? It's hard. They said they'd give me that welfare so I can get treatment. They won't even give me that.

What else can I say, honey, it's hard! I sold everything in the house. I don't have anything left. Open the door over there, so he can see! Everything I had, I sold. What else can I do? If I wasn't indebted to those Gypsies, it'd be different. But now, I can't be thinking about the treatment when they come to my door asking for money. What else can I do? What else can do? I'm dying here.

(*One month after this interview, Margareta Avadanei died)

4

Il Consigliere

Nae Butuc: A Don Quixote with only three front teeth, thin, and with the ends of his moustache moving up and down with every word. Although he is Romanian, he is the local head of the Roma party and the council member representing the Roma at the mayor's office. You can always find him under his umbrella at one of Buhusi's outdoor cafes. He says he is the protector and friend of the Mocirlans, their link to the mayor and the police. "A money lender, a loan shark, a crook, and a middleman for departures abroad – for a price," he is described by Buhusi's deputy mayor Vasile Zaharia, and even by some of the Gypsies in the community.

I'm fighting to change our image a little, because there are a lot of untrue stories about Mocirlans. It all starts with poverty. There used to be a community of Roma here, right next to our city, that lived with us in the factory. As Buhusi was a monoindustrial city, once the industry fell, everything fell – and from there started the westbound mass migration. I, being Romanian, was working for a company, in supplies and retail, where Gypsies were assigned the lowest-level jobs. That's how I met them. After the Revolution, when the factory began to fall apart and they started to understand hardship, when everyone was creating parties and sub-parties, of course they were open to all those problems and organized their own party.

Now I am the Roma's council member at the Buhusi mayor's office, but I come across the same situations as any council member. There is a law, Law 430, that forces mayors to hire us: all community presidents have to be on the mayor's payroll, so we can go to the communities and know how to talk to people in their language, so we can protect their interests…The problem is that mayors are not too sympathetic when it comes to these Roma communities.

It bothers me when I knock on the mayor's door, and I feel he won't help me. But he does help me, because he knows I have the Gypsies backing me and I can very easily start another Hadareni (a violent dispute between Romanians and Gypsies). These people are capable of anything to prove they're right. When they're wrong, they're wrong. I'll give you another example, to base it all on examples: I took five men to jail; five men that had been wanted for three years; after a few talks, they turned themselves in a month later. They went into the chief's office on their own, drank a shot each, and said, "Chief, take us to jail."

So, it's very painful, but I did that too.

But when they're right, they're right. I have a very good friend who's the manager of a security agency for the Bacau Hydroconstruction Company, that after all the floods, took up a four-year project along the Bistrita River.

He asked me to give him 35 people from Mocirla. Last winter, he worked with three of our people and he was satisfied. But these guys have full criminal records. Even in communist times they had trouble with the police. They were the scapegoats. For the times they've been right and for all the injustices committed against them, Hadareni should be a myth.

Their problem is this: what they did was six, eleven, twenty years ago. Romanian law stains you and doesn't clean you. Do you understand, sir? The chief gave me an idea and I think I'll take him up on it, but it's going to be a little hard. Here it is: for everyone who has been in jail, I, as local Roma party leader, have to sue the Romanian government and win their rehabilitation. I have to do this soon. If I want to guarantee these 35 jobs, I have to do it. Thirty-five salaries in their communities mean a great deal.

These people are honest by nature. You just have to live among them. To feel them, to understand them. When I'm upset, I come here, I meet up with them, I talk to them, I joke with them, I climb up the hill on this side, they take me with them, I come back down on the other side, and I go home happy.

Mr. Catalin, let me explain to you because I know them best: evil and hate come from inside. For 100 years or more, I don't know how long they've been here, they've been marginalized and stigmatized as Gypsies, Mocirlans, thieves, bandits, wretches, or whatever else they call them. At the factory, the work they did was for much smaller salaries than of the Romanians, because they didn't have an education; very few of them made it. But the authorities didn't take the person into account: Tincoi, or Aurel, or Catalin.

Now we have to be patient, very patient.

First of all, I help them become legal. Identity cards, birth certificates, passports for those who want to leave, all those things…from A to Z, starting with the departure. And when they get there, I keep in contact with them, I take their phone numbers. Everything.

When they want to come home, they call me, I send a driver, they come back. I have a contract with an agency in Bacau that is especially for them. I work very well with the police, I go to them almost every week. And when he can, the chief, Mr. Chirilou, who is an extraordinary chief, comes here.

If somebody has a problem here, with the mayor, with the police, with anything, I tell them what to do. But I don't just send them, I go with them personally and take care of it. I am their president. When they make mistakes, I take them to jail. When they don't, I defend them.

(* Butuc was beaten up by some Gypsies and was no longer wanted in the Swamp)

5

The Young Mother

A woman with inquisitive eyes, with neck length red hair which reveals her round, yellow earrings fluttering in the wind, is sitting at the gate, hands on her hips, half hostile, half gentle. 'It smells like food here, I just made a stew. It would be nice if I could live in the other house but the water got in and it smells like mould. Just don't say that if you came to the Gypsies, we are less developed and we don't know how to receive guests'. Gabriela Stan, 35 years old, is a tenacious tigress running her own home and her 4 children (the eldest is in 9th grade) with an iron hand. She returned from Italy two years ago to take care of her children, her husband is still there and he sends them money every month; she is hoping to leave as soon as possible to Sicily.

Why are those in charge not fixing these roads? I wouldn't want a street like the main road but at least a bit of tarmac so the kids would not get stuck in the mud on their way to school. They should not discriminate us, because we are Gypsies and they are Romanians. We have the same heart, the same eyes, the same mouth.

This world is evil. Wherever we go, we don't get priority because we are Gypsies. I used to work at a factory until I got fired in 1998. I got out on a decree. I also received 7 million lei (210$). My husband is still in Italy. I was there for two years. I returned for the children because they are all grown up now and I need to make a future for them. My husband stayed there. But I hope that we can all go back if we find some work for the children. I don't know how we would have managed if we wouldn't have left.

We only got the money from social care 3 or 4 times. Everyone would tell me that I have a cow, that I have a horse. I don't know if the cow or the horse gave me money for the basics: meat, potatoes for the children, whatever, if the cow could only say „here", and put some money in my pocket. People judge badly here. They are very envious. The mayor especially, he upsets everyone. This world is too wicked and I wonder why God is keeping us on the face of the earth.

While I was in Sicily, I worked really hard for very little money. Whoever loves to work wouldn't say no, but whoever doesn't… I used to make formaggio (cheese), just as you make cheese here, from morning till dawn I was burned by the fire, they were very hospitable people, but very close-fisted.

I got 150 euro and my husband, Viorel, got 350 euro as he was working more. They got paid more. And they wouldn't like to hire one of their Italians, who doesn't work like us, for 500-600 euro. And I would get a gift every time they saw I was too smart, too clean and too exaggerated, so, in a way they wanted to see if I was Gypsy: but I would tell them my origin, I give you my word that I didn't want them to know.

I don't know, someone came with us and told my boss: 'I think this girl is one of those who wear long skirts… And I said: this is not true. They would always ask about the long skirted ones. I don't know, I have no idea. So I was acting smart. Because I worked together with the people in the factory and I know how people are. I wouldn't tell them I was Gypsy because nobody would accept me. Many women left this place and started talking, swearing, doing what you're not supposed to do, selling themselves for money, even for 5 or 10 Euros, so…

And they started calling us Gypsies. I was not ashamed that I was Gypsy, but I was afraid of losing my job. If those people found out, they would have fired us on the spot. But the Romanian is still a Romanian. You're looked down upon because you are Romanian, and looked down upon even more because you are Gypsy.

When someone came and said 'zingari (Gypsy in Italian) are dangerous, they ammazza persone (kill people)', when I heard that…. I thought I would lose my job. And look, to this day, my boss does not know that I am a Gypsy, she calls me at home, she speaks to me, she sends money for the girl. Now my husband sends money, 500 euro per month, but they are of no value to us, he works on a construction site and does really well, he never imagined he would be able to find such a good job. He has been there for 4 years and he already makes 1200 euro per month and we hope he will find something for the children, but something less demanding, I mean, I wouldn't want to work them too hard at such a young age.

Romeo, come here! He is the eldest, in the 9th grade. I have four children: Romeo is 16, Ionut 15, Cosmin 11 and Bianca 8.

I raise my hand at them sometimes, I hit Romeo yesterday. He wants to go out and do whatever he likes, but I don't agree. I don't like seeing him going around, like a bum, being messy, causing trouble. If you want to make a future for yourself you have to work. Romeo is in the 9th grade, he doesn't even know how to write his own signature. I don't even send Ionut to school. He fights with other children, doing crazy things. I told him: you are better off at home.

I wouldn't want to break their bones from this age. All that we do, we do for them. We want to lift them up because they are children. I have a husband who's too good to be true and four amazing children. I will work for my children.

My boss, the one I talk to on the phone, she promised me that soon it will be easier with all the paperwork… This is what we hope: to leave.

6

The Pub Owner

*C*oming down from Mocirla, a little to the left,
there's old Sava's place. It used to be called "At
the Happy Gypsy." Now everyone just calls it
"At Sava's." After last night's scene, the pub owner
should have bags under his eyes. But morning brings
the same calm, rested face. When you see old Sava, a
gentle, quiet man of 50, you can't imagine that the
night before, he flew out from behind the counter
like a hawk among the brawlers and smacked some
sense into the fiercest one. Maybe it should be
pointed out that many of old Sava's clients are
wanted criminals…

"I threw them out, the bastards…They're young, I've been in surgery. Otherwise, if I didn't have this hernia surgery, I'd cane them. That's their nature. When there's a scene, Romanians don't come running, but the Gypsies…A Romanian won't jump to save you. Even if someone's about to kill you, they won't get involved. The Gypsies are united, they come running right away, they defend each other, even if they're enemies. When a Romanian beats up a Gypsy, the whole hill comes running.

Well, they don't get drunk every night. But, every now and then, I'll call the police, 'cause that's the only way: they're bad. Last night, my wife called the cops. They were disturbing the peace. They got off easy. They put it on their record and gave them a 2 million lei (60$) fine. But then they don't come here anymore. They go up the hill. I told the woman, "Leave them alone, let them go to hell, 'cause they're dangerous. You'll be one of their enemies. They've been to jail. They're losers. You don't know what to expect from them. They're poor, they don't have anything, but they're mean too, let them go to hell!"

We keep coming down on them…and one day they'll surprise you 'cause they're capable of anything, they have nothing to lose. The woman's brave, but fights mostly with words. She doesn't have a bad heart. But she can't bring them down 'cause they're goddamn fierce.

I've had this booth for about 12 years. Before, I worked as a driver for a merchandise truck, for IRTA. But this new job, ever since I opened the shop, is a lot harder. You saw how easy it is to make trouble.

7

The Old Lady

A *handkerchief is pulled over the teary eyes of a tiny, tiny, old lady, with skin like black, cracked clay. At 84, Iona Gruia is the oldest in Mocirla. At 14, she started working at the Felt Factory in Buhusi and didn't leave until she was old. Her husband died on the Russian war front. She lives alone, she has a 4 million lei monthly pension, she eats when she's hungry, mostly beans and potatoes. At night, she doesn't sleep much, and cries over the ruined world. It used to be different...*

Come on in, honey, come on in. Welcome. Excuse the mess, I can't cope anymore. I say it with fright and shame, honey: I'm weak now. And I don't have anyone to rely on. What am I supposed to do with the 4 million (120$) from my husband, dead on the Russian front? You buy food, honey, you buy anything, honey, and, it's hard.

In Ceausescu's time it was different. There was bread the size of my head, there was food, salami was 9 communist lei (2,5$) per kilo, fish 7 communist lei (2$) per kilo. Now there's so much hunger, honey. I make a pot of soup today and I'll have it 'till tomorrow. What else can I do? I wake up in the morning, I sweep, I tidy up, I put another pot of beans on the fire 'cause I need to cook myself some food.

I send these girls down to the valley sometimes to buy food. I eat beans and potatoes most of the time, 'cause there's no money for anything else. I'll make a bowl of beans, I'll have it for two days. Like I eat a lot?! You can't, when a barrel of wood is 2 million (60$). Everything's more expensive. I heard the cigarettes people smoke are 40,000 lei (1,2$)!

Poor Ceausescu didn't know what else to give, to widows, to orphans. He was good, the poor man. He would see you in a store and ask you: do you have money or not? No? Give her this, give her that; he'd fill your purse. He was good, honey, Ceausescu.

I was born in 1921. I was around during Antonescu's time. And when I was born, there were a lot of Gypsies in Mocirla like now. They worked in the factory. The factory was a pot of gold for all of Mocirla. My parents were at the factory too.

I didn't go to school. I went straight to the factory. When I turned 14, some guy, Cretu (Curly), came to the door, a business man. He went around asking "You have land? No. You have land? No." He rounded up maybe 100 people, men, women, children and he took them to the factory. The people that didn't have jobs, he took them to the factory. Dad went to the mayor's office, he gave some money, and they wrote me down as 15 years old so I could work. I got into the factory, thank God, the Virgin Mary, and St. Paraschiva.

I got out when I was old. This was my friend – this stick. We would all wait for each other and come home. There weren't cars or buses back then. And we wouldn't go around with boots or shoes in the mud. Nooo, you had your slippers and the men had their moccasins and their pants, honey, and you walked to the factory in the mud, flip-flop, until it drove you crazy.

At five in the morning I would leave home. And I'd be at the factory at 6, 6:20. But I had a good boss. Sometimes I'd come with my feet all wet. You didn't have time to eat. If a pipe was thin, or empty, he'd call you back. I worked 'till I'd burst. But I'd get 1,200 communist lei (360$). And I built the house on my own, without my husband, 'cause he died in the war. The house is from about 1950.

I worked for 30 years. I didn't steal so much as a string 'cause mom had eight kids and I was afraid of getting fired and starving to death. And that's how I ended up anyway. But now I'm weak.

If there were factories now – What did that Iliescu do? He disfigured the people! – would you see these kids outside? To the factory, honey! But now, where can they go? Where can they go? A bunch of them went to Italy. Gypsies, Jews, Hungarians, all kinds of nationalities left. They leave out of hunger, honey, for work. To the pigs, to the sheep, wherever they can, to the olives, everywhere. You go anywhere out of hunger.

Well, when you get old, you don't sleep like you used to…I can't sleep at night.

It's light in the house, I look around, honey, the dog barks at those devils that broke my fence, these criminal kids: they throw rocks, bottles, jars. My fence is their hangout, it's where they meet. From eight to twelve. Every night it's a madhouse. They'll break your head if you come between them. You won't even know what hit you when they throw a rock or a bottle or a jar. And they bend over the fence. Crazy kids. It wasn't like this in my day, honey. You couldn't just talk to a girl at night in the street. Her parents would snap your neck! When a boy would come to talk to you, he'd go to your parents first. It's a mess now, honey. My, my, my. They see all that nonsense on TV. I don't have a TV. I don't even want to see or hear any of it.

The world's gone crazy, honey. Girls want to wear their skirts up to their thighs, honey. Well, in my day if you parents saw you like that, or wearing pants, they'd snap your neck like a chicken. My, my, my! It was long skirts, loose, like the Gypsies. It was good. That was the life. You wouldn't see women with their heads uncovered, or with lipstick, or with their nails done. That was the life. A kid of 14, 15 would be in the factory. A boy like you would be a factory boss. The world is ruined, honey! It's not like it was. Ask anyone.

8

"The Italian Woman"

She stands next to the table, restless. She taps her fingers on the table or twirls her beautiful hair, dyed red. Cornelia Stan - 31, with two kids, separated from her husband, pretty, vivacious, blue eyed, with a fast tongue - is waiting to go back to Sicily, to her rich, 40 year old Italian. She was there last year, but the carabinieri caught her and sent her back.

If you want to go to Italy, there's Romica Poian with transport. It is more expensive – 300 euro with customs in Austria and everything – but they take you to your destination. They take care of your passport, here in Buhusi, or wherever you're from.

But if you don't have a job secured there, it's better if you just don't leave.

I stayed there six months, and I wouldn't leave the house out of fear of being caught by the carabinieri. As soon as I went out, they caught me. They ask, "Do you have sogiorno?" If you don't, they put you in a van, they take you to the police station, and ask: mother, father, family, everything. Then they put you in a car and take you to jail. I was in jail for two weeks. It's kind of a migration center with Romanians, Chinese, Italians, Germans, all nationalities. They give you food, clothes, everything. After two weeks, they take you to the airport and they send you back to Bucharest with a ban: you can't go back. But you can go back: you have a civil union with any man and you can pass. On a bus, in two- three days you're there.

It's hard. The first time I cried, oh my God! And if you have one of those Italian dictionaries, you pick up the language in no time. It will take you less than a month. Anyway, I'm leaving again. I was there with a 40-year-old Sicilian, and now he calls me, we talk. He has money, and land. He would come here with his car, but he doesn't know his way around and he's afraid of Romania, of being killed. In the end, if he did come, and he had money, I'd kill him myself. I'll find other Italians, now that I know the language.

But I'll go to him. I have my man, I don't need money, I don't need anything. My mom told me, "Better a good whore than a bad housewife. If you want to live, girl, go after him. Be smart. Don't leave any tracks, don't leave anything behind." I'm leaving in a few months. I'll pay the driver and he'll leave me in Tributina, in Rome. From there I'll take a van from Tibutina to Catania. And then, I'll call my Sicilian on the phone and he'll come and get me, ciao, arrividerci.

9

The Teacher

*I*t's 6.30 am. Bundles of smoke-colored fog descend from the surrounding ghostly hills. Gabi carefully ponders her every step, zigzagging through fresh cow dung, but her small Cinderella-shoes often sink in the muddy alleyways. Even though she doesn't live in Mocirla but on the neighboring hill, the mud is just as deep. When she gets to the road, she washes her black shoes in a pond and keeps walking towards the school. Gabi Gruia, 29 years old, is a Romani language teacher at the Buhusi Arts and Crafts school. She has a 4.5 million lei salary. She is the only one in the community who went to college, in Bucharest. She lives between two worlds and neither one accepts her completely: she is the intellectual of a Gypsy community with which she cannot identify,

while wider society, labels her, even if not openly, as
a Gypsy.

Please don't write about me. I don't like it. I
usually don't like being praised. I don't want people
to look at me like an animal at the zoo just because I
am the only one in the community who went to
college. What's the big deal? I simply want to be
treated like a normal person. My friend, a Romanian
language teacher, why doesn't anyone praise her
because she finished college? It just feels like
something normal to me.

I don't dress like a Gypsy, I don't act like a
Gypsy. But sir, I am a Gypsy! If you want to accept
me for who I am, good. If not, that's fine too. I don't
have Gypsy friends. Not even the ones I'm friendly
with. It'd be normal for me to feel comfortable
around my own kind, to be one of them. But I can't.
And it's hard for them too, to accept that one of them
can rise above. If you rise above them, it's like they

have something against you, because you succeeded and they didn't.

They're afraid of me. I can tell when they talk to me that they're holding something back. They think I have a lot of acquaintances and powerful connections. I think that maybe the only solution would be for these people to be displaced, scattered among the Romanians, a family here, another one there, in different cities, among civilized people. For someone to give them jobs, houses, etc., so they can do what they see their neighbors doing.

Just about everyone around here has seven, eight children. In Bistrita, near here, a family named Buhoi has 12 children. The schoolteacher from over there was telling me that she met with their mother, pregnant in the hospital. She had a mangy kid, with snot around his nose. She asked her why she doesn't wash the child. "Listen lady, instead of washing this one, I'll just make a clean one," she answered.

We can't change the world. We have to adapt and move on. I'm not an idealist like I used to be. At school, I know I won't be able to help these children. Before, I was different. I thought I could change them, to save them from this swamp. Now, I've given up.

This year, after teachers' strike, and with what Prime-minister did to them, I decided to leave the country. I'm going to go to Italy.

Final picture

Limbos and another seven or eight men were at old Sava's pub again last night, gathered around a 1$ bottle of liqueur. They were celebrating one of their returns from Italy: a very big guy, with a tight shirt, with a mean face, with expressionless, predatory eyes that looked you right in the brain. Then, another one came down from the hill, with clay on his head, dead tired. He had worked all day at sticking together a house with clay for 3$. And with that 3$, he bought everyone drinks: "Drink up guys, 'cause now I have money!" The conversation that followed was hypothetical – although the most frequently pronounced word was "fuck" – about what was better: to steal and cash in big all at once or to work honestly for almost nothing?

Alone, the one that came from the clay, the one that defended working, the one that was made fun of, left, bowing his head and saying, more to himself, "Whatever. Better I stay here and work than take it in the butt from everyone in jail…"

They hang around like this all the time, fierce, joking.

Rich Roma, Poor Roma

*T*he same hunter-gatherer instincts, in the same
"transitional" social conditions, may lead to
opposite results.

Dan "Finutu" died in august 2012 in a car
accident. His palace in Buzescu is a faithful replica
of the Caracal Court (the only court of law that ever
caused trouble for Finutu). Ciprian Limbos from
Mocirla neighborhood of Buhusi, spent two years in
jail for a pack of underwear. Finutu's wealth is
estimated at 4 million euros, Limbos is dirt-poor.

Buzescu is one of the richest Gypsy
communities in Romania, Mocirla lives hand to
mouth on stealing, welfare and money sent by
relatives abroad. The demise of Ceausescu marked a

crossroads for the Roma population: while some got rich by fishing the troubled waters of transition, most sank in poverty. What made the difference between the rich Roma and the poor Roma?

Romanian Gypsies have met freedom twice: in 1855-56, when slavery was abolished, and in 1989, when the communist regime fell. Both then and now, most of them got badly burnt, but some fared marvelously. In both cases, Gypsies massively migrated toward the West. Between 1977 and 1983, the last 65,000 nomads and semi-nomad Roma were settled under a PCR program. Local authorities were forced to provide housing and employment for them. During the dark years between 1980 and 1990, a part of the Roma population went back to their traditional lifestyles, but in modern forms.

The Gypsies became specialists of the black market. In 1989, they were already well-versed. "After the revolution, even a stupid person could build five villas buying and selling metal", says Marin Nicolae, a former boiler maker in Buzescu.

Romania emerged from communism with a technology perfect for being sold for scrap. People started collecting and trading in scrap metal. Capitalizing on the absence of any regulation in the field, hundreds of thousands of pieces of equipment were cut up to be exported as scrap metal. Even power line towers, railroad tracks or manhole covers were stolen. It was only in 2001 that the Emergency Order no.16 was published - and approved by Law no.456 – , regulating recyclable waste management.

"My son is also in Bucharest, he's staying at the Intercontinental", Gica from Buzescu, living across from Dan Finutu, told me.

It was around 1993 in Alexandria, Teleorman, where I spent my school years. I was applying to the School of Journalism and looking for lodgings in Bucharest, and he had come to my father to buy some doors for the palace he was building. I recall two things from that conversation: that Gica didn't want to pay with money, but with gold, and that he mentioned his boy who "was staying at the

Intercontinental Hotel" – the biggest and most expensive hotel in Bucharest at that time.

The Buzescu Gypsies were already fabulously rich then, and I couldn't understand why. I understood it, after spending some time in the Gypsy community of Mocirla, Buhusi. Those Gypsies also had the extremely alive hunter-gatherer instincts that had helped those of Buzescu gain from the regime change. But the Moldavian Romas lacked the mastermind, the astute leader to understand and unite them around the opportunities created by the old regime burial, turning a handful of poor people into an organized and dangerous mafia worthy of Kusturica's "Black Cat, White Cat".

Gypsy Clans

Why and how are Gypsies divided into clans

In the past decades, more and more Gypsies have forgotten or have begun to ignore the tribes they belonged to. A third of the Roma in Romania no longer define themselves as members of a particular clan, according to a 1992 study by sociologists Elena Zamfir and Catalin Zamfir. Most of those who still consider themselves part of a clan are: settlers (13,8%), braziers (5,9%), woodworkers (4,5%), tin workers (3,7%), silk weavers (3,2%), bear trainers (2,7%), brick layers (1,5%), Gabors (1,4%), and florists (1,2%).

As in India the family profession was, as a rule, inherited and practiced in the family – the

secrets of the trade passed down from father to son –
the majority of the Roma clans have been formed,
some since the migration towards Europe, around
various occupations with which Gypsies earned their
living.

The main Gypsy clans in Romania and their characteristics.

Blacksmiths

• Occupation: Manufacturing of iron tools and objects.

• History: They held a monopoly over iron manufacturing throughout the Romanian Medieval Ages. In the 20th century, many became farmers, industrial laborers, or construction workers. After 1989, few blacksmiths who remained in the towns still make wagons and tools.

• Characteristics: They were wealthy Gypsies, among the first to settle down, but also among the first to lose their language. The majority of their descendants have lost their Gypsy identity.

Tin Workers

•   Occupation: Tin-coating the pots and dishes of pension owners around whose houses they would periodically settle; begging.

•   History: After collectivization, the majority became farmers.

•   Characteristics: They are the descendants of the Turkish Roma. They were among the poorest Gypsies; they traveled in tilt-wagons pulled by oxes.

Bone Carvers

•   Occupation: They manufactured objects from animal bones (ex. combs, handles, ornaments).

•   History: After industrialization decreased demand for their products, the bone carvers became mainly trash collectors or dealers of feathers or kitchen plates.

• Characteristics: Bone carvers are the descendants of Indian ivory workers.

Braziers

• Occupation: Manufacturing of buckets, pans, pots, alembics, glasses, etc. from brass foil or, more recently, from aluminum.

• History: From the beginning, they lived in tents, traveling in colored wagons. Many have maintained their traditional lifestyle until very recently. Of all the Gypsy clans, they were the last to settle down.

• Characteristics: Among the braziers, the position of bulibasa (chief) is maintained and the kris (trying) is still practiced by the community elders.

Woodworkers

- Occupation: Searching for and working of gold, carving of softwood, berry picking.

- History: From the end of the 18th century, when finding gold became increasingly difficult, the woodworkers dedicated themselves more and more to wood-carving.

- Characteristics: Woodworkers are the descendants of the old Indian goldsmiths; they are known as bath makers, spoon makers, and dish makers.

Settlers

- Occupation: Various jobs for boyar courtyards or monasteries; agriculture.

- History: Gypsies "of the hearth" were tied to the land before slavery abolition and the 1864 agricultural reform. Several decades after the emancipation laws, the notion of "settlers" became synonymous with "sedentarization." Many Gypsies without trades or plots of land entered the settlers' family.

•	Characteristics: The Roma "of the hearth" were the first to lose their traditional language and way of life. The settlers are the most integrated within the majority of the population.

Fiddlers

•	Occupation: Music

•	History: The fiddlers are a clan that detached themselves from the settlers in the middle of the 20th century.

•	Characteristics: The fiddlers from rural settings played at celebrations and were farmers by day. In the city, they were more specialized and lived easier lives. Some of the most talented became renowned musicians.

Florists

•	Occupation: Flower commerce

- History: They are a relatively new clan which appeared in the interwar period.

- Characteristics: They are the most homogenized, and relatively rich, Roma category.

Bear trainers

- Occupation: Training bears.

- History: Their forefathers were magicians, trainers, tightrope walkers, etc. During the Middle Age, they wandered through towns and cities with trained bears, earning a living from shows. After the profession disappeared at the beginning of the last century, bear trainers learned the trades of other clans.

- Characteristics: After settling down, they formed relatively compact groups, maintaining their language and tradition.

Gabors

- Occupation: Commerce, tinsmithing, modern professions.

- History: They are Roma from Ardeal who took their name from the landowner of the estate on which they worked.

- Characteristics: They do not have a specific trade.

Copers

- Occupation: Commerce with horses.

- History: although it almost disappeared, their clan slowly came back to life in the last 15 years, mostly in Arad, Brasov and Braila counties.

- Characteristic: They were specialized in the "youthening" and healing of horses.

Silversmiths

- Occupation: Gold and silver decorations manufacturing.

- History: Excellent craftsmen, they represented the elite of the Gypsy clans. Today there are very few left in Bucharest and ,Teleorman, Ialomita, and Tulcea counties.

- Characteristics: Within the community, traditional trying and marriage is still practiced.

TIMELINE: SHORT HISTORY OF ROMANIAN GYPSIES

On the Bed of Procust

Throughout the centuries, Romania's faces and society have shaped the Gypsies.

In the Middle Ages, although enslaved, most Gypsies remained nomads after their arrival in Romanian territory, scouring the country in hoards – on established routes – to win their keep with their crafts. They would spend the winters on their masters' estate and pay an annual tribute.

The progressive boyars who freed them through the emancipation laws of the mid 19th century wanted to settle them, turning them into tax-paying peasants. After the 1864 agrarian reforms, Gypsies became small land-owners. Yet many refused the land, taking instead advantage of their newly-acquired freedom to resume to nomadic lifestyles.

Between 1942 and 1943, Marshal Ion Antonescu, convinced that he was ridding the country of parasites, deported to Transnistria 25,000 nomadic and sedentary Gypsies with no means of support, or who had been charged with various offences. Only 10,000 survivors returned to Romania in the spring of 1944.

The communists wanted – and succeeded for the most part – to turn the Gypsies into laborers, integrating them, sometimes forcefully, into modern lifestyles. Officially, Gypsies were no longer considered a separate ethnicity; they were sent to school, and were guaranteed jobs and houses. The turmoil following 1989 was a crossroad for the Roma population who went in two opposite directions: while some took advantage from the old regime's burial, most of the others slid down a slope of inescapable poverty.

Short History of the Romanian Gypsies

• 1385 – The first documented recording of Gypsies on Romanian territory. Dan the First, ruler of Wallachia, gives to the Tismana monastery, among other gifts, 40 homes for the Gypsies.

• 1855–1856 – The abolition of Gypsy slavery, both in Moldova and Wallachia.

• 1855–1880 – A few decades after the emancipation, the seasonal variations of traditional nomadic lifestyle turn into chaotic vagabondage. The second great Gypsy migration towards the West begins.

• 1900–1940 - Traditional Gypsy professions begin to decline, facing competition from advancing industries. A Gypsy intellectual elite emerges, calling for the "emancipation and reawakening of the Roma people."

- 1942 – 1944 – 25,000 Gypsies are deported to Transnistria.

- 1977 – 1983 – The last 65,000 nomadic and semi-nomadic Roma are forcibly settled due to a PCR (Romanian Communist Party) program. Local authorities are ordered to secure them with housing and jobs.

- 1980 –1990 – After the economic crisis, a part of the Roma population returns to the traditional way of life, but with a modern twist. These Gypsies become specialists of the black market.

- After 1990 – Ion Cioaba, Octavian Stoica and Nicolae Bobu are the first three Gypsies to be elected to Parliament.

Postface: One million Zorbas

By Cristian Lascu, Editor in Chief of the Romanian edition of National Geographic Magazine.

On a gray winter day, we were descending from the Apuseni Mountains. We got to the Huedin railway station, only to discover that we had missed the train for Bucharest. The next one was due in 7 hours. Shipwrecked with us in the freezing waiting room, a few other passengers: peasants staring blankly; a couple of workers eating bacon and onions on a greasy newspaper; an old woman dozing with a knapsack in her lap.

We tried to nap while time was slowly dragging on. After a while, the door broke open and a gust of blizzard pushed in three Gypsies. I could notice the audience promptly backing away in distrust. Not a bit intimidated, one of the Gypsies took out a violin, another one an accordion and started playing their tunes and dancing. They challenged us. A bottle passed from hand to hand. The small room suddenly warmed up and before we knew it time had passed.

I met many Gypsies in Romanian villages, perfectly integrated in their communities. Almost all of them exquisite musicians. Leaving aside their stealing and mobbing, I admire them for their great capacity to adapt, for their solidarity and especially for the simple and deeply human zest for living. Among us live close to 1 million Zorbas.

The End

That's me in the center!

Injured during a friendly soccer game with the Gypsies, I was taken uphill, to a medicine man from Mocirla to fix my hand. After half an hour of painful tries, I fainted. The next day, in Buhusi hospital, the hypothetic luxation proved to be a serious fracture.

Photo by Bogdan Croitoru

For more photos from the Swamp go to www.bogdan.croitoru.com

DEAR READER,

I hope you enjoyed this book!

Would you do me a small favor?

I'd love to hear from you and what you thought of this book!

If you could take a few moments, click on the link below and write a blurb on Amazon about this book.

Your feedback will help others to learn about this book and help me learn how I can better serve my readers.

[Click here to leave me a review on Amazon.com](#)

You can reach me at www.catalingruia.com or on Facebook

Like me on Facebook: www.facebook.com/ByCatalinGruia

Thank so much, I hope to hear from you and I wish you all the best!

Catalin

About the Author

Catalin Gruia is a veteran journalist who has written and reported for the Romanian edition of National Geographic for over 10 years. He is currently Editor in Chief of National Geographic Traveler and Deputy Editor in Chief of National Geographic Romania.

International awards

- **First prize (Geographica section)** at the International Seminar of National Geographic International Editions, Washington, 2004

- Johann Strauss Golden Medal, Vienna, 2010;

- Kinarri Trophy, Friends of Thailand Awards, Bangkok, 2013;

ALSO BY CATALIN GRUIA

The Man They Killed on Christmas Day

The Rise and Fall of Saxon Transylvania

What About Dracula? Romania's Schizophrenic Dilemma

Who Were The Dacians?

Printed in Great Britain
by Amazon

26334036R00051